THE BILL OF RIGHTS
THE FIRST AMENDMENT: THE RIGHT OF EXPRESSION

BY RICH SMITH

SERIES CONSULTANT: SCOTT HARR, J.D. CRIMINAL JUSTICE
DEPARTMENT CHAIR, CONCORDIA UNIVERSITY ST. PAUL

VISIT US AT
WWW.ABDOPUBLISHING.COM

Published by ABDO Publishing Company, 8000 West 78th Street, Suite 310, Edina, MN 55439.
Copyright ©2008 by Abdo Consulting Group, Inc. International copyrights reserved in all countries.
No part of this book may be reproduced in any form without written permission from the publisher.
ABDO & Daughters™ is a trademark and logo of ABDO Publishing Company.

Printed in the United States.

Editor: John Hamilton
Graphic Design: John Hamilton
Cover Design: Neil Klinepier
Cover Illustration: Getty Images
Interior Photos and Illustrations: p 1 Constitution & flag, iStockphoto; p 4 KKK march, Corbis;
p 5 protest rally, Getty Images; p 7 George Lincoln Rockwell, Getty Images; p 9 Constitution & flag
detail, iStockphoto; p 11 facade of U.S. Supreme Court, iStockphoto; p 13 *Freedom of Worship* by Norman
Rockwell, National Archives; p 14 portrait of Thomas Jefferson by Rembrandt Peale, Library of Congress;
p 15 children praying, Photospin; p 17 *Freedom of Speech* by Norman Rockwell, National Archives;
p 19 Tinker family, Corbis; p 20 soldier saluting flag, iStockphoto; p 21 children saying Pledge of
Allegiance, AP Images; p 22 Condoleezza Rice testifying, AP Images; p 23 co-editor Liz Teigen, AP
Images; p 25 anti-war rally, AP Images; p 27 NAACP rally, AP Images; p 29 blogger Sean Dustman,
AP Images.

Library of Congress Cataloging-in-Publication Data

Smith, Rich, 1954-
    First Amendment : the right of expression / Rich Smith.
        p. cm. -- (The Bill of Rights)
    Includes index.
    ISBN 978-1-59928-914-4
    1. United States. Constitution. 1st Amendment--juvenile literature. 2. Freedom of speech--United
States--Juvenile literature. 3. Freedom of religion--United States--Juvenile literature. 4. Freedom of
the press--United States--Juvenile literature. 5. Petition, Right of--United States--Juvenile literature. 6.
Assembly, Right of--United States--Juvenile literature. 7. Freedom of association--United States--Juvenile
literature. I. Title.

KF4770.Z9S65 2008
342.7308'5--dc22
                                        2007014570

CONTENTS

INTRODUCTION

Below: A child participates in a Ku Klux Klan rally. The First Amendment guarantees freedom of expression, even if that expression seems wrong to most people.

Suppose you and a group of your friends decide one day to have a parade through the center of town. Some of those in your group play musical instruments, so they can form a marching band. Others are good at building things, so they can make a float. The rest can carry flags and banners and wave at everyone standing on the sidewalk along the parade route.

Then you realize your parade needs a name. You decide to call it "The Parade For World Peace." You call it that because all the music and floats and flags and banners will be about world peace.

Do you have a right to hold a parade that calls for world peace? The answer is yes, you do.

Now, suppose you decide instead that the name of your parade will be "The Parade For World Rule By The Ku Klux Klan." Suppose too that the planned route of this parade will go through a part of town that is home to large numbers of racial minorities. And that all your friends marching in the parade will be wearing white hooded robes. And that the banners and flags and floats and music will be about "white power."

Do you have a right to hold a hate-filled parade that calls for the KKK to take over the planet? Once again, the answer is yes, you do.

How is that possible? Parading for world peace is good, but parading for the KKK is hurtful. How can the police and others in government allow something so plainly wrong as a Ku Klux Klan parade?

In the United States, both of these parades, with their very different messages, are allowed because of the right to freedom of expression.

Freedom of expression means you have the right to say or write or sing or draw or play-act what you believe or feel. It is your right as a citizen of the United States, even if what you want to express is truly horrible and offends people.

This right of free expression is spelled out in the First Amendment to the Constitution of the United States. The Constitution is a document that describes how the U.S. government is set up and operated. It also explains the job of the president, the lawmakers of Congress, and the people who work as judges.

At the end of the Constitution are 26 additional instructions for the government. These are called amendments. The first 10 make up what is known as the Bill of Rights. The Bill of Rights lists the special freedoms every human is born with and is able to enjoy in America. Also, the Bill of Rights tells the government that it cannot stop people from fully using and enjoying those freedoms unless the government has an extremely good reason for doing so.

Above: Freedom of expression is the first, and some say most important, part of the Bill of Rights.

ALLOWING SPEECH WE HATE

ONE OF THE MOST FAMOUS First Amendment cases involved a 1977 lawsuit filed by the National Socialist Party of America against the Chicago suburb of Skokie, Illinois. It is a good example of how the First Amendment protects even speech that a majority of people don't like.

The National Socialist Party of America was formerly known as the American Nazi Party. The members of this group believed almost everything that Adolf Hitler of Germany had believed. That included extreme hatred of Jews.

In 1977, the National Socialists applied for a permit to parade through the heart of Skokie. Skokie at the time was home to many, many Jews. Some of them were survivors of the death camps that Hitler had forced them into during World War II.

It was no surprise when the village of Skokie refused to give the National Socialists a parade permit. Skokie officials feared violence if the Jewish residents and the parading Nazis caught sight of one another.

In response, the National Socialists asked the courts to rule that Skokie had denied the party its First Amendment free speech and assembly rights. The U.S. Supreme Court agreed with the National Socialists and ordered Skokie officials to let the party march through the village. The Court also ordered the village to allow the paraders to wear their favorite Nazi-style uniforms and freely display swastika flags and banners.

The Supreme Court's ruling also said that the party even had a right to hand out pamphlets filled with rage against Jews and others. The justices said this because ideas cannot be made illegal under the First Amendment. Not even ideas that people don't like and can't stand.

Above: George Lincoln Rockwell, former leader of the American Nazi Party.

Four Freedoms in One

The United States Constitution's First Amendment declares that "Congress shall make no law respecting an establishment of religion, or prohibiting the free exercise thereof; or abridging the freedom of speech, or of the press; or the right of the people peaceably to assemble, and to petition the Government for a redress of grievances."

You might have noticed four different types of freedoms named in the amendment:

- The first is freedom of religion.
- The second is freedom of speech.
- The third is freedom of the press.
- The fourth is freedom to demand that the government stop doing wrong.

These four liberties are grouped together in the First Amendment because they all are forms of a more basic freedom. That basic freedom is the right to believe the way you want. The freedom to have your own beliefs is also known as freedom of thought, freedom of conscience, and the right to an opinion. Freedom of belief is said to be the one right that most helps you shape your future and find true happiness in life. That is why freedom of belief is the only right that is absolute and can never be limited by government. It can never be limited because government never has a good reason for preventing people from thinking.

Facing page: A copy of the United States Constitution, next to a U.S. flag. The first part of the Constitution is called the Preamble. It introduces the Constitution and its purpose. It states: "We the People of the United States, in Order to form a more perfect Union, establish Justice, insure domestic Tranquility, provide for the common defense, promote the general Welfare, and secure the Blessings of Liberty to ourselves and our Posterity, do ordain and establish this Constitution for the United States of America."

We the People of the

insure domestic Tranquility, provide for the common defence,

and our Posterity, Do ordain and establish this Constitution f

Article I.

Section. 1. All legislative Powers herein granted shall be vested in a Congress of the United States, which shall consist of a Senate and House of Representatives.

Section. 2. The House of Representatives shall be composed of Members chosen every second Year by the People of the several States, and the Electors in each State shall have Qualifications requisite for Electors of the most numerous Branch of the State Legislature.

No Person shall be a Representative who shall not have attained to the Age of twenty five Years, and been seven Years a Citizen of the United States, and who shall not, when elected, be an Inhabitant of that State in which he shall be chosen.

Representatives and direct Taxes shall be apportioned among the several States which may be included within this Union, according to their respective Numbers, which shall be determined by adding to the whole Number of free Persons, including those bound to Service for a Term of Years, and excluding Indians not taxed, three fifths of all other Persons. The actual Enumeration shall be made within three Years after the first Meeting of the Congress of the United States, and within every subsequent Term of ten Years, in such Manner as they shall by Law direct. The Number of Representatives shall not exceed one for every thirty Thousand, but each State shall have at Least one Representative; and until such enumeration shall be made, the State of New Hampshire shall be entitled to chuse three, Massachusetts eight, Rhode Island and Providence Plantations one, Connecticut five, New York six, New Jersey four, Pennsylvania eight, Delaware one, Maryland six, Virginia ten, North Carolina five, South Carolina five, and Georgia three.

When vacancies happen in the Representation from any State, the Executive Authority thereof shall issue Writs of Election to fill such Vacancies.

The House of Representatives shall chuse their Speaker and other Officers; and shall have the sole Power of Impeachment.

PLENTY OF CONFUSION

Something you might have noticed about the First Amendment is that the authors used just 45 words to write it. That's not many words at all. A student would probably use more words explaining to a teacher why he or she was late for class.

The reason the First Amendment is so short is that the authors wanted to keep it simple. They thought this would help people more easily understand it. They did not want people of the future to get into arguments about what was meant when the amendment was first written.

But it did not quite work out that way. There have been plenty of arguments through the years about what those 45 words mean and what limits they place on people's freedom and on government power.

A good way to understand why people argue over the First Amendment is to look at one of the most familiar rules of your school: No running in the hallways. That rule is simple and would seem to be easy to understand. But you or your classmates might wonder if that rule applies only when the hallways are filled with students. If so, you might then wonder how many students actually have to be in the hallway in order for it to count as being filled. You might also question how fast you have to be moving through the hallway before it can be said that you are running and not merely walking very fast. And is running something you do on two legs only? What if you are speeding along on your hands and knees? Is the student who uses a wheelchair breaking the rule by traveling at running speed, even though he or she has no legs to move? And would the rule against running still apply if your safety is put in danger by a giant boulder that suddenly appears at the far end of the hallway and races toward you?

The way you would get answers to these questions is by asking your school's principal. The way people get questions answered about the First Amendment is by going to court and asking a judge. Many times the final answer doesn't come from the first judge asked. In those cases, the final answer comes only after the question works its way up to the highest court in the land. The U.S. Supreme Court is the highest court. It has given lots of answers over the years to questions about the First Amendment. Those answers shape our understanding of the First Amendment today.

Below: The facade of the United States Supreme Court building in Washington, D.C.

ESTABLISHMENT OF RELIGION

The First Amendment begins by promising freedom of religion. That promise is divided into two parts, which are called clauses. The first of these is the Establishment Clause. It says that the government cannot establish an official religion for the United States. There was an official government-made religion in Great Britain at the time the United States was born in 1776. It was the Church of England. People in those days who refused to join the Church of England were usually prevented from having good jobs and nice homes. In earlier times they were jailed and even put to death by the government. The Founding Fathers of the United States did not want the same problem here. So the first limit on government power in the Bill of Rights was a ban against the creation of a Church of the United States.

The U.S. Supreme Court has said that the Establishment Clause also means the government cannot favor one religion over another. For example, Congress cannot pass a law allowing Christian churches to pay no taxes, and then tell Jewish synagogues and Muslim mosques that they must pay taxes. If a law applies to one church, it must apply to all churches.

The second part of the First Amendment's freedom of religion section is the Free Exercise Clause. The idea here is that the government must not prevent people from praying or going to a house of worship or taking part in the rituals of their faith. But the Supreme Court has said that government may pass laws limiting the free exercise of religion. An example of such a limit is the law that makes it illegal for a man or woman to be married to more than one person at a time. Some religions believe marriage involving two or more wives or husbands at the same time is perfectly fine. The formal word for that is polygamy. However, government believes it is best for the nation and for society if a person is married to just one other. The formal word for that is monogamy.

As the Supreme Court has explained, the Free Exercise Clause speaks of both the freedom to believe and the freedom to act. The freedom to believe cannot be limited. But the Supreme Court says limits can be placed on the acts inspired by those beliefs.

Left: Freedom of Worship by Norman Rockwell.

SEPARATION OF CHURCH AND STATE

YOU MAY HAVE HEARD people talk about the separation of church and state. This refers to the Establishment Clause of the First Amendment. The words "separation of church and state" are not actually in the First Amendment. They appear instead in a letter written in 1802 by President Thomas Jefferson to church leaders in Connecticut. The church leaders were worried that government might someday tell them how, where, and when to worship God. Jefferson said not to worry because the First Amendment was like a very tall wall and it would do a good job protecting churches from government interference.

The understanding of what Jefferson meant by "separation of church and state" changed over the long years that followed. Now, people and the courts take him to mean that the wall is there to do the opposite by protecting government from church interference.

This newer view of "separation of church and state" helped the U.S. Supreme Court in 1962 decide to abolish the custom of public schools starting their day with an assembly in which students said prayers led by either a teacher or a school official. One year later, the High Court told schools they also had to stop requiring students to worship at the beginning of classes by reading from the Bible.

In 1971, the Supreme Court changed its mind a little. It decided it was constitutional after all for schools to allow students to read from the Bible, but only if they were using it as a history, literature, or social studies textbook. More recently the Court ruled that prayer and worshipful Bible readings could take place on public school campuses as long as they are done by students on their own and do not disrupt the school.

Facing page: Children praying in a church.
Below: Thomas Jefferson, by painter Rembrandt Peale.

FREEDOM OF SPEECH

The framers of the First Amendment felt that America's survival depended on people being able to learn truth. They understood that people armed with the truth are people who can make wise decisions about their lives and about all other matters. They believed that the best way for people to learn truth is by having as few limits as possible on what can be said or written. That is why in the United States you can say almost anything you want. *Almost* anything. Among the things you can't say are words that can cause serious harm to people or that can make people want to riot. Such words are called "fighting words."

A basic rule of life is that things change as time goes by. That is true whether you are talking about cars or about clothing styles or about tastes in music. Even ideas change with the passing of time. So have people's opinions about what a fighting word is. For example, the worst thing you could have called someone 100 years ago was a liar. That was a fighting word back then. Today you can call someone a liar and it usually is no big deal. The Supreme Court was aware that today's fighting words can become harmless ones tomorrow. So it came up with a test that the government could use to decide if a word was a fighting word or not. You knew it was a fighting word if it was likely to cause the person who heard or read it to become angry enough to hit the person who said or authored it.

The idea that there can be fighting words that the government has a responsibility to prevent comes from a 1942 Supreme Court ruling in the case of *Chaplinsky v. New Hampshire*. It all started when a street preacher named Walter Chaplinsky was stopped by a New Hampshire town marshal from speaking to a gathered group of people. The preacher was angered by that. He then insulted the lawman by cursing at him. That led to the arrest of the preacher. The preacher sued and claimed that neither New Hampshire nor any of its towns had the power to prevent him from saying what he said to the marshal. All nine members of the U.S. Supreme Court agreed that Chaplinsky was in the wrong because his words were meant to injure.

Facing page: Freedom of Speech by Norman Rockwell.

There are at least two other types of speech the government can put a stop to. One is called libel. This refers to lies told about someone for the purpose of hurting that person or ruining his or her reputation. The lies have to be put in writing in order to count as libel. The term used for lies that are spoken is slander. Speech is not libel or slander if the words used are truthful and are not meant to injure.

Libel can be committed against one person or against many. Libel against many is known as group libel. It is also known as hate speech. The U.S. Supreme Court in 1952 ruled in favor of the state of Illinois in a very important case about group libel. The state had a law making it illegal for anyone to say or write bad things about people of a different ethnicity or who lived in poverty. A white man by the name of Beauharnais made up a pamphlet to urge that blacks not be allowed to buy homes in white neighborhoods. His pamphlet included terrible and hurtful lies about Americans whose ancestors came from Africa. He was arrested for that and later found guilty. Beauharnais sued to have his conviction thrown out on the grounds that his First Amendment rights had been violated. The U.S. Supreme Court said no. Beauharnais' rights had not been violated, the Court said, because he had committed group libel.

Another type of speech the government can halt is speech that poses a "clear and present danger" to others. An example of this is when a man seated in a crowded theater creates a panic by falsely shouting that a fire has broken out in the building. This could cause people to be trampled and seriously injured or even killed as terrified members of the audience climb over one another to reach the exits. Something like this may or may not have ever happened. But it was used by the U.S. Supreme Court in explaining its 1919 decision in the case of *Schenck v. U.S.* It was in the middle of World War I that Charles T. Schenck penned a leaflet to protest the draft. The draft is where people are ordered by the government to serve in the military. Schenck held the opinion that the draft was illegal. He was arrested and convicted of trying to hurt America's war effort by urging people to ignore the draft. His case went to the U.S. Supreme Court, where it was decided that the government has a duty to curb evil speech.

The Supreme Court 50 years later had a different view of things when it decided the case of *Tinker v. Des Moines Independent Community School District*. John Tinker was 15 years old when he and his 13-year-old sister Mary Beth and their classmate Christopher Eckhardt came to school wearing black armbands to show that they were against the war in Vietnam. This was after the Des Moines, Iowa, board of education had made a rule that students could not wear protest armbands. School officials saw the armbands on the three students. John, Mary Beth, and Christopher were suspended from school. Their parents sued the school district. The long legal battle that followed ended with the U.S. Supreme Court deciding that the First Amendment rights of the students had been violated by the school. The Court said that the school had the power to forbid the armbands only if wearing them were likely to disrupt classes.

Below: Members of the Leonard Tinker family learn of the 1969 Supreme Court decision allowing the children to wear black anti-war armbands to school. From left to right: Lorena, Paul, and Mary Beth Tinker.

CAN YOU BE FORCED TO SALUTE THE FLAG?

MANY STUDENTS BEGIN their school day by standing to salute the American flag and saying the Pledge of Allegiance. But they do not have to do so. They can remain seated and silent if they choose. A 1943 U.S. Supreme Court decision said they have this right under the First Amendment. That case was *West Virginia Board of Education v. Barnette*.

Schools today sometimes forget *West Virginia Board of Education v. Barnette*. That's what happened to Alabama high school student Michael Holloman. One morning in 2000, a classmate got in trouble for not saying the Pledge of Allegiance. The next day, Michael showed support for his friend by likewise not saying the pledge. He also raised a defiant fist high in the air. The teacher scolded him and a school official spanked him with

Below: An Army soldier salutes the U.S. flag.

a paddle. Michael was humiliated. He sued his school in federal court. The judge ruled in favor of the school. But Michael took his case to a higher court and won. The judges of the 11th U.S. Court of Appeals said that Michael had every right to do what he did because of *West Virginia Board of Education v. Barnette*.

The attorney for the school tried to win by showing Michael's actions were disruptive and hurtful to other students. This was very clever. The attorney knew that First Amendment rights are limited. He knew that in some situations the government can deny people a little of their rights in order to stop disruption and hurt. But the appeals court found that Michael's actions were not disruptive and hurtful enough for the school to deny him his free speech and free expression rights.

Above: Kindergartners recite the Pledge of Allegiance at Florence Markofer Elementary School in Elk Grove, California.

Freedom of the Press

The news media play a special role in protecting democracy. They tell voters about the individuals who want to be elected as government leaders. They tell readers, listeners, and viewers about wars, the economy, new medicines, and many other developments that can affect people's lives.

The news media also investigate and uncover wrongdoing by government officials and agencies. These investigations are important because they help pressure government to be honest and fair. But government leaders do not particularly like being investigated by the press. Many leaders would, if they could, stop reporters from telling the public about government wrongdoing that has been uncovered. But the First Amendment prevents them from stopping the reporting of such news.

It is called censorship when the government stops news from being reported. Government censorship of the news was common in the years before America broke away from Great Britain in 1776. There were no radio or television or Internet news services in those days. But there were printing presses where newspapers,

Below: National Security Advisor Condoleezza Rice gives testimony before the commission investigating the terror attacks of September 11, 2001.

books, and pamphlets were produced. Colonial printers were issued licenses for their presses, and nothing could be legally printed without censors first looking it over to make sure it did not paint a bad picture of the government.

The First Amendment generally does not allow government censorship of the news. But there are a few situations where censorship is permitted. One involves news published in a school-sponsored student newspaper. This became a settled matter in the late 1980s when journalism students at Hazelwood East High School near St. Louis, Missouri, sued their principal for blocking publication of a school newspaper story about girls on campus who had become pregnant and another about parents who were going through a divorce. The principal feared that the girls and parents who were named in the stories would be hurt by what was written. The students' lawsuit went all the way to the U.S. Supreme Court. The justices took the side of the principal. They said he did the right thing in this situation. They said he had a very good reason for censoring the two news stories.

Above: Liz Teigen, co-editor of the Independent Kodak student newspaper published for students at Everett High School, in Everett, Washington.

FREEDOM TO PETITION AND ASSEMBLE

The government of the United States is given the job of protecting the people who live in this country. Sometimes the government does not do enough to protect the people. Other times it does enough but goes about it in the wrong way. No matter what, it makes people angry when the government lets them down.

People who grow angry about government can tell Congress, the president, and the courts how they feel. They can write a letter. They can send a telegram or an email. They can pick up the telephone and call. They can write an article for the newspaper or be a guest on a television talk show. They can make a movie. They can do any of these without fear that the government will respond by sending the police to arrest them. The right to complain to the government is what the freedom to petition for a redress of grievances is all about.

Petitioning the government is something you can do on your own as an individual or with the help of others. A large gathering of petitioners is called an assembly, and the right to do that is also protected by the First Amendment. In fact, the U.S. Supreme Court believes petitioning and assembly go hand-in-hand. The High Court first took that view in 1876 with its ruling in a case known as *United States v. Cruikshank*. The Supreme Court was even more sure of things in the 1939 case of *Hague v. CIO*, when it said that the Constitution guarantees the right to assemble so that information can be shared and people's views about important national issues can be voiced.

Under the First Amendment, government cannot stop an assembly just because officials don't like the message that the people want to send. Marches and sit-ins are to be allowed. The only thing government can do is control the time of day the assembly occurs, the place it happens, and the way it all unfolds. It can do this because government has a duty to make sure an assembly does not tie up traffic in the streets, block the sidewalks, or prevent people who are not part of the assembly from freely going in and out of buildings. This is why people who protest at abortion clinics can freely do so, but can be required to stay some distance away from the clinics' doors.

Below: An anti-war demonstration held in Washington, D.C., in March 2007. The First Amendment gives the right to petition and assemble, even if the government doesn't agree with the message.

FREEDOM TO ASSOCIATE

In addition to the four First Amendment rights, there is a fifth right that is not actually written into the First Amendment. It is understood to exist because the other freedoms of the First Amendment all hint at it. This unwritten fifth liberty is the freedom of association.

Freedom to associate means you have the right to get together with other individuals who share your ideas, values, interests, or goals. This freedom was put to a very difficult test during the time of the civil rights movement. A number of cities and states in the late 1950s passed laws ordering the National Association for the Advancement of Colored People (NAACP) to let local government officials peek at the names and addresses of NAACP members. The government said it only wanted this information to help the NAACP pay less in taxes. But the real reason was to frighten members into quitting the NAACP and to scare away anyone who wanted to join the organization. Government leaders hoped that they could destroy the civil rights movement by harming the NAACP. The U.S. Supreme Court stepped in and ruled in 1960 that the states cannot force an organization to reveal who its members are if that would hurt freedom of association.

Even so, freedom of association is not an absolute right. For example, the U.S. Supreme Court has stated that it is not a violation of a grown-up's right to freely associate if a dance club for teenagers won't allow him or her to enter. The 1989 case in which this was decided is *Dallas v. Stanglin*. The city of Dallas, Texas, passed a law allowing teen-only dance clubs to open. A man named Stanglin, who owned such a club, wanted the courts to toss out the city law so that his club could be enjoyed both by teenagers and adults at the same time. The U.S. Supreme Court said that freedom of association did not apply in this case because the 1,000 or so teenagers who usually came to Stanglin's club were not organized into an association and they did not meet to discuss issues of public importance.

Facing page: Members of the NAACP demonstrate in Washington, D.C., urging the hiring of more minority law clerks at the U.S. Supreme Court.

The Questions Keep Coming

The First Amendment. So very short in length, but so very packed with importance. And constantly being put to the test. In the future, experts in constitutional law believe that the First Amendment will be tested as never before. This is because there are more and more new ways to spread ideas and information. Internet podcasting, blogging, and file sharing are just three examples of these new ways. Each of them raises questions about First Amendment rights.

For example, look at blogging: is it personal speech or is it more like newspaper reporting and deserving of the kind of special protections given to the press? Can bloggers be guilty of libel if their hurtful words are erased from the Internet five minutes after first being posted? Can the work of bloggers be censored by the government? How will the rights of bloggers to write what they want be balanced against government's need to protect young children from information and images that can harm them?

All of these questions and many others will have to be answered by the courts with the help of Congress and the president. The work will be hard. But the good thing about the First Amendment is that it was designed to stretch so that it could cover situations never imagined when it was created more than 200 years ago.

Facing page: U.S. Navy Corpsman Sean Dustman poses with his blog "Doc in the Box," displayed on his desktop computer screen. Dustman has written reports from several tours of duty in Iraq. Blogs and other "new media" increase the ways we communicate with each other. Military blogs such as Dustman's have become a major supplement to mainstream media, such as print and television. The protection given to blogs under the First Amendment has yet to be fully determined.

INDEX